# The Best Dancer

Story by Annette Smith

Photography by Lindsay Edwards

"I love dancing,"
Rani said to Mum.
"I'm the best dancer
in my class."

"You will have to dance for us
at home," said Mum.

At home,

Rani looked in the kitchen.

"I can't dance for Mum and Dad

in here," she said.

"And I can't dance in here,"

she said.

"The big table and chairs

are all in the way.

Where can I dance?"

"Rani! Come out here!" said Dad.

"Grandma has come to see us."

Rani went outside to see Grandma.

"Hello, Grandma," said Rani.
"I'm the best dancer
in my class."

"Let us see you dance, Rani,"
said Grandma.

Forsyth Road Elementary School

Rani looked at the little table and the flowers.

"Dad," she said.

"Please help me with this table."

"I will dance for you out here,"
said Rani.
"I'm going to get dressed
for my dance."

Rani went inside
the house again.

"Here I come," said Rani.

And she danced and danced and danced.

"You **are** the best dancer,"

said Grandma.

"I love to dance, too."